DY

THE ART OF MODERN LIFE I

DYNAMISM

is sponsored by
British Alcan Aluminium plc

CONTENTS

Front cover
C R W NEVINSON *Dance Hall Scene* c1913-14

SPONSOR'S FOREWORD

When the Albert Dock buildings were so imaginatively restored in the mid 1980s, British Alcan Aluminium was delighted to supply cast aluminium windows to replicate the Victorian cast iron originals. Now, we are equally delighted to be associated as sponsors with this exhibition by the Tate Gallery of the North.

Alcan is one of the world's leading aluminium producers and has manufacturing units throughout the United Kingdom. In the north west of England we have aluminium extrusion plants at Warrington, St Helens, and Workington. We have chemical plants at Widnes and at Clifton Junction near Manchester, where we also produce magnesium casting alloys.

Currently we are building Europe's first dedicated recycling plant for used aluminium beverage cans at Warrington. This will help reclaim some 50,000 tonnes of aluminium per annum and enable charities to raise several million pounds by assisting in the collection process.

We have a policy of encouraging the visual and performing arts throughout the country and particularly in those areas where we have a strong manufacturing presence. That is why it seemed particularly appropriate for us to support the work of Liverpool's new and exciting gallery by sponsoring two of its major exhibitions for 1991.

D M Ritchie
Managing Director, Chief Executive Officer
British Alcan Aluminium plc

PREFACE

This is the first of the annual displays to have been presented on the ground floor of Tate Gallery Liverpool which does not show a recognised art historical grouping. *Dynamism* looks across national and art-historical boundaries at what artists in Europe had in common. In the years before the First World War they all experienced the effect of new technology on the pace of modern life. Although these effect have been variously examined under national groupings such as Vorticism, Futurism and Rayonnism, the present display aims to highlight the sources of inspiration which they shared, rather than delving into the complicated histories of each group.

In this aim we have been enormously helped by the loans made available by the Imperial War Museum, and we are grateful to David Penn, and particularly to Martin Garnett, for the time they have given to collaboration with Tate Gallery Liverpool. These loans highlight not only the presence of new technology, but also the parallels between art and machinery in terms of style and shape. A particularly clear example of this fusion is in Jacob Epstein's 'Rock Drill', and we are fortunate to be able to show the reconstruction owned by Birmingham City Art Gallery.

Although, inevitably, the National Collection of Modern Art in Britain is strongest in its holdings of the English art movement Vorticism, *Dynamism* intends to focus on a period that is remarkable for its internationalism. It is salutary to remember, however, that the machinery which united the interests of so many artists in the years before the Great War was put to such divisive and destructive effect after 1914.

Nicholas Serota
Director, Tate Gallery

Lewis Biggs
Curator, Tate Gallery Liverpool

THE DYNAMISM OF MODERN LIFE

Penelope Curtis

Absolute Motion plus Relative Motion Equals Dynamism.
Umberto Boccioni

The years before the Great War in Europe saw tremendous technological changes, accompanied by as many changes in mental attitudes. There was a new consciousness of the 'dynamism' of modern life. In different arts, in different countries, artists sought ways to represent speed and its effects. Often their efforts involved the shattering of old methods of representation. While artists began to reinvent perspective, poets experimented with fragmented syntax and composers with atonal music. The Futurists in Italy, the Vorticists in England, the Rayonnists in Russia, and the Simultaneists in France were all inspired by the pace of modern life to find new ways to represent it on the canvas.

Through Cubism artists had already begun to become accustomed to the idea of drawing on all kinds of contemporary thought. The idea of 'Dynamism' – perpetual becoming – had been discussed by the French philosopher Henri Bergson in his 1907 book *Creative Evolution*. The poet Guillaume Apollinaire introduced Bergson's emphasis on constant change into French art criticism. The Futurists saw 'Dynamism' as an important part of their programme, and they explained how to achieve it. F T Marinetti proclaimed 'We achieve an absolute dynamism through the interpenetration of different atmospheres and times', and the sculptor Umberto Boccioni wrote 'The gesture which we would reproduce on canvas shall no longer be a fixed *moment* in universal dynamism. It shall simply be the *dynamic sensation* itself'. Art was now about more than simply seeing, it was about experience and physical sensation. The poet Blaise Cendrars affirmed in a poem from 1913, 'The windows of my poetry are wide open onto the boulevards'.

URBAN LIFE

We exclaim, the whole brilliant style of modern times – our trousers, jackets, shoes, trolleycars, motorcars, airplanes, railways, grandiose steamships – is fascinating, is a great epoch.
Mikhail Larionov and Natalia Goncharova, *Rayonnist Manifesto*, 1913

A consciousness of the awesome scale of urban life, along with the social pleasures it offered, began to intoxicate the world of fine art in this period. Although England had been predominantly urban for some time, the experience was much newer for France and Italy. Social experiences such as department stores, sport, the circus, the music hall and tea-dances all enjoyed a heyday in the pre-war years, becoming subjects of great interest for artists. In advertising – 'the flower of contemporary life' as Cendrars called it – art and life came together. Part of the appeal of these new phenomena was in the large numbers of people they brought together. The individual merged with the crowd, fusing with the rhythms of the city.

Cinemas multiplied, so that there were, for instance, 200 cinemas in Paris by 1913. This new interest in the excitement of urban pleasures, and the urban crowd, was examined by contemporary psychologists, and expressed by writers such as Paul Adam in his *The Mystery of Crowds*, Emile Verhaeren in *The Soul of the City*, Réné Arcos in *The Tragedy of Spaces*, Alexandre Mercereau in *People of There and Elsewhere*, and H-M Barzun in *The Era of the Drama*.

In a single glance
I wrap up the earth
Occident, Orient, both hemispheres – all the globe!
Bathed in daylight and night.
H-M Barzun, *La Terrestre Tragédie*, 1907

The force of the crowd was promulgated by Jules Romains who published a *Unanimist Manifesto* in

1905, and *La Vie Unanime (The Unanimist Life)* in 1908. He voiced his impression that 'the life of civilized man has assumed a new character', due to 'The present tendency of the people to mass together in the cities;...ties stronger and more binding (are) established between men by their duties, their occupations, their common pleasures; an encroachment, even greater, of the public on the private, the collective on the individual'. Romains believed that these new facts would inevitably lead to a new expressive creativity. 'I strongly believe that the bonds of feeling between a man and his city, that the whole ethos, the large movements of consciousness, the colossal passions of human groups are capable of creating a profound lyricism or a superb epic cycle'. Unanimist sentiment marks the early stage of Futurism, when the style was more symbolist, before it had been marked by Cubism.

> *...The young factories!*
> *They live heartily.*
> *They smoke higher than the peal of the bells.*
> *They are not afraid to hide the sun,*
> *Because they create sun with their own machines.*
> *Like a dog shaking itself on leaving the sea,*
> *The foaming factory scatters around itself*
> *Drops of energy which wake the city.*
> Jules Romains, *L'Eglise*, 1908

Despite his pseudo-scientific tendency, Jules Romains is often linked to the Abbaye de Créteil brotherhood which was set up outside Paris by the artist Albert Gleizes and the writer Alexandre Mercereau in 1906. However in their interest in the dignity of the worker the brotherhood was perhaps closer to Tolstoy and Morris, and more interested in the potential of collective life as promised by Verhaeren, than in Romains. Nevertheless, they did see their circle as 'An expression of our time...of electricity, motor cars, factories', and Romains was certainly published by the Abbaye press. His influence seems especially apparent on Marinetti, who was himself a lay-member of the group.

JOHN MARIN *Downtown, New York* 1923

C R W NEVINSON *Dance Hall Scene* c1913-14

ALBERT GLEIZES *Portrait of Jacques Nayral* 1911

The motorcar lives off obedient explosions
It makes the surrounding space reverberate
The people in the car, elbow to elbow,
Bathed in speed, lose their weight there.
Jules Romains,
Dynamisme III: The rays which cannot be seen

The Abbaye combined an interest in the possibilities of the modern world with an interest that was much more cosmic, deriving from more traditional spiritualism. The poet Jacques Nayral, who was related to Gleizes, was particularly interested in psychic research. In this way dynamism parted company from real life, and moved into a spiritual search not represented in this display. Beyond Wassily Kandinsky, and his text *On the Spiritual in Art*, we move into the more complete abstraction of Kasimir Malevich and Piet Mondrian.

OH BLAST FRANCE

pig plagiarism
| BELLY
| SLIPPERS
| POODLE TEMPER
| BAD MUSIC

SENTIMENTAL GALLIC GUSH
SENSATIONALISM
FUSSINESS.

PARISIAN PAROCHIALISM. Complacent young man,
so much respect for Papa
and his son !—Oh !—Papa
is wonderful : but all papas
are !

BLAST

APERITIFS (Pernots, Amers picon)
Bad change
Naively seductive Houri salon-
picture Cocottes
Slouching blue porters (can
carry a pantechnicon)
Stupidly rapacious people at
every step
Economy maniacs
Bouillon Kub (for being a bad
pun)

Page from *Blast* 1 1914

BLESS ENGLISH HUMOUR

It is the great barbarous weapon of
the genius among races.
The wild **MOUNTAIN RAILWAY** from **IDEA**
to **IDEA**, in the ancient Fair of **LIFE.**

BLESS SWIFT for his solemn bleak
wisdom of laughter.

SHAKESPEARE for his bitter Northern
Rhetoric of humour.

BLESS ALL ENGLISH EYES
that grow crows-feet with their
FANCY and **ENERGY.**

BLESS this hysterical **WALL** built round
the **EGO.**

BLESS the solitude of **LAUGHTER.**

BLESS the separating, ungregarious

BRITISH GRIN.

Page from *Blast* 1 1914

THE ART OF MAKING MANIFESTOS

the precise accusation, the well defined insult
F T Marinetti, 1909-10

Marinetti was the leader of the Futurists. He established methods of promotion which have been taken up and used by artists to the present day. One of his most important platforms was the manifesto. Manifestos had of course existed before Marinetti, and indeed there was quite a flurry at the turn of the century, with Saint-Georges de Bouhelier's *Naturist Manifesto* (1897), Jules Romains' in 1905 and E L Kirchner's *Programme for die Brücke* (1906). However Marinetti's advised combination of violence and precision was new. The art became the manifesto, the manifesto became art.

On 20 February 1909, Marinetti announced *The Foundation and Manifesto of Futurism* on the front page of *Le Figaro*. A group of artists gathered round him to implement his ideas, announcing their development through a further series of manifestos signed at first by Carrà, Boccioni and Russolo, and then by Severini and Balla as well. *The Manifestos of Futurist Painters* was published in February 1910, and read in March from the stage of a Turin theatre. It was followed by *Futurist Painting: Technical Manifesto* and manifestos on Futurist sculpture, music, cinema and architecture.

The Vorticists and the Rayonnists followed the Futurists' example in manifesto-making. Apollinaire's *Antitradition Futuriste Manifeste-synthèse* (1913), which was published in France and Italy introduced the alternate curses and blessings (MER . . DE/ROSE) which were taken up with such vigour by the Vorticists in their own magazine.

Cover of Marinetti's *Zang Tumb Tuuum*

INTERNATIONALISM

Marinetti had published his 1909 manifesto on the foundation of the Futurist group in Italy in a Paris newspaper; it was published in the Russian press shortly afterwards, and he gave a reading of it in London in April 1910. Extracts were published in England that summer. The *Manifestos of Futurist painters* was published in the French magazine *Comoedia* in 1910. Marinetti made a general propaganda tour of European capitals in the winter of 1909-10, and may even have gone to Moscow and St Petersburg at that time. In 1910 Gleizes was selected by Mercereau for the *Knave of Diamonds* exhibition in Moscow. The French poet Apollinaire wrote for the Italian magazine *Lacerba* and was the Futurists' French contact. From February 1912 a Futurist exhibition circulated Europe, beginning at the Bernheim-Jeune Gallery in Paris, and moving on to London, Berlin, Brussels, Hamburg, Amsterdam, The Hague, Frankfurt, Breslau, Dresden, Zurich, Munich and Vienna. The Sackville Gallery catalogue published the 1909 manifesto and the 1910 *Technical Manifesto*. Gino Severini, an Italian Futurist who lived in Paris, had a one-man show in London in 1913. Marinetti began to acquire a cult following in London where he performed in concerts such as the *Grand Futurist Concert of Noises* at the Coliseum and where the *Daily Mail* published his manifesto *The Variety Theatre*. In April 1914 the Doré Galleries in London mounted a large Futurist exhibition. Marinetti made a performance piece called *Zang Tumb Tuuum* about his time as a war reporter in the Balkan War of 1912 which was given in performance in London, Paris, Berlin, Moscow and St Petersburg.

There were also links between Munich and France, and Munich and Russia. Munich had long been the natural magnet for Russian artists – which meant that there were strong links between the Russian 'Futurists' such as Goncharova and Larionov and the Russians in the Blaue Reiter group in Germany – though Paris began to take over from Munich around 1906. The French painter Robert Delaunay became very close to the Blaue Reiter group and he exhibited in Munich and Berlin (along with Boccioni). One can also cite

Russian links with the English, for Zinaida Vengerova interviewed Ezra Pound for the Russian journal *Strelets,* and the painter Wadsworth translated Kandinsky's *On the Spiritual in Art* for the first edition of *Blast* in June 1914.

In Berlin the magazine *Der Sturm* acted as a focus. Apollinaire wrote for it, and Boccioni's *Futurist Painting – Technical Manifesto* was published there. The editor of *Der Sturm,* Herwarth Walden, was also instrumental in organising the international art shows that ended with the war. His Autumn Salon of 1913 showed work from fifteen countries, mixing the Delaunays, Gleizes, Balla, Boccioni, Severini, Goncharova and Larionov with Mondrian, Klee, Kandinsky, Arp and Ernst.

SIMULTANEITY IN SPACE & TIME

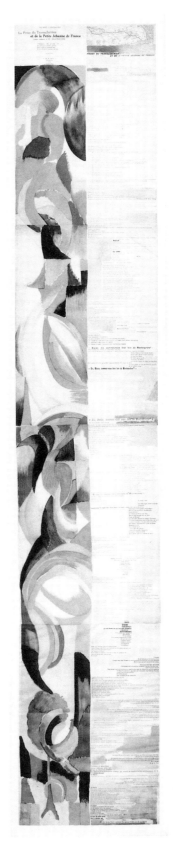

La Prose du Transsibérien, the collaboration between the poet Blaise Cendrars and the painter Sonia Delaunay which is exhibited here, was published in *Les Hommes Nouveaux* in 1913. Its subtitle was 'poems, simultaneous colours, in an edition reaching the height of the Eiffel Tower: 150 numbered and signed copies'. This 'first simultaneous book' unfolded like an accordion to a length of over two metres. The Eiffel Tower has a height of 300 metres. The text of the poem is preceded by a Michelin railway map of the Trans-Siberian journey from Moscow to the sea of Japan.

The poem takes its readers, along with its 'French' protagonists, far from home. We should however remember that many 'French artists' were not actually French. Sonia Terk grew up in St Petersburg; Cendrars was born in Switzerland, and lived in St Petersburg and New York before Paris. The world was not just becoming smaller in poetry; it was in fact. Proof of this was that the Poem itself was exhibited in Paris, Berlin, London, New York, Moscow and St Petersburg in the autumn of 1913.

All this was made possible by enormous progress in transport. The Trans-Siberian railway was completed in 1905. The Trans-African and the Trans-Andine railroads are of the same period. By 1910 you could buy a combined rail and sea ticket that could take you round the world in forty days.

C R W NEVINSON *The Arrival* 1923- 24

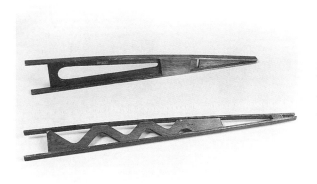

First World War aircraft wing ribs

Moreover, you did not need a passport. Simultaneity allowed for multiple experiences to come together. Ease of transport meant that one could see, as Cendrars did on his train journey in poetry across Siberia, cuckoo clocks from the Black Forest, coffins from Malmö, and corkscrews from Sheffield. And from the train windows the whole of Europe could be seen.

> *The force of steam, the lines of the express, of gas, of*
> * oil,*
> *This triumph of our age, the Atlantic cable wire.*
> *The Pacific Railway, the Suez Canal, the tunnels*
> * under Mount Cenis, Saint-Gothard and Hoosac,*
> * the Brooklyn Bridge.*
> *This earth quite wrapped up by railways, by*
> * steamship lines which cross all the seas…*
> Blaise Cendrars

The same pre-1914 period saw the successful expeditions to the two Poles, and the first flights over the Alps and across the English Channel. 'England is no longer an island' quipped the pilot Louis Blériot in 1909. It also saw the first use of aeroplanes in war. The aeroplane fascinated poets and artists in France and Italy especially. Telegraphs and telephones became much more common, as did the automobile, whose use increased thirtyfold in the decade before the war. In 1904 radio signals began to be sent from a single antenna installed at the top of the Eiffel Tower. In 1913 it transmitted the first signal round the world.

> *Eiffel Tower*
> *Heavenly Guitar*
> *Your wireless telegraph*
> *A magnet to words*
> *Like a rose to the bees.*
> V Huidobro, *Tour Eiffel,* 1918

> *The Eiffel Tower comes and goes at the top. The sun,*
> *a cloud, a mite is enough to make it longer, or make it*
> *shorter. The metal bridges are just as mysterious and*
> *sensitive. Watches set themselves. From all sides ocean*
> *liners approach their ports of call. The semaphore*
> *signals. A blue eye opens. The red closes. Soon there*
> *is nothing but colours.*
> *Co-penetration.*
> Blaise Cendrars, *Profound Aujourd'hui,* 1917

GINO SEVERINI *Suburban Train Arriving in Paris* 1915

A belief in Simultaneism suggested a collage-like technique to artists. The collapsing of distance and time zones brought previously distant objects together, bringing out the deep analogies between things. It could also, and particularly in Futurism, make for a layering of memories and motifs. Futurist Simultaneity fused the physical and mental worlds, aiming at, as Boccioni wrote in 1912, 'the synthesis of *what one remembers* and of *what one sees*'. Early Futurist paintings, before around 1912, sought especially to capture moods and evocation: 'The simultaneousness of states of mind in the work of art: that is the intoxicating aim of our art' they proclaimed in the Sackville Gallery catalogue. Simultaneism also ended an egocentric view of the world – the obsessive 'I' – and focused on scientific interpretations. Bergson's notion of 'psychic duration' was picked up by the Futurists, who liked to put a scientific gloss on things, in addition to being deeply impressed by contemporary scientific theorizing.

The time in Paris the time in Berlin the time in Saint Petersburg and the time in all the stations…
Blaise Cendrars, *La Prose…*, 1913

Newspapers asserted simultaneity in time and place, reporting as they did, on one page, events happening all over the world. Apollinaire claimed for poets the freedom enjoyed by the press to be everywhere at once. Marinetti also noticed this new availability of diverse experience: 'An ordinary man can, in the space of one day, travel by train from a little dead town of empty squares, where the

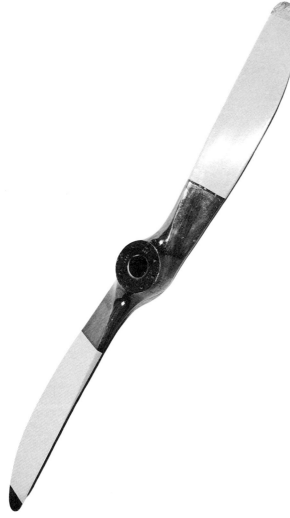

First World War aircraft propeller

Metal components produced during the First World War

sun, the dust, and the wind amuse themselves in silence, to a great capital city bristling with lights, gestures and street cries. By reading a newspaper the inhabitant of the mountain village can tremble each day with anxiety, following insurrection in China, the London and New York suffragettes, Dr Carrel, and the heroic dog-sleds of the polar explorers. The timid, sedentary inhabitant of any provincial town can indulge in the intoxication of danger by going to the movies and watching a great hunt on the Congo... Then back in his bourgeois bed, he can enjoy the distant, expensive voice of a Caruso.'

SIMULTANEITY IN ART

Modern man registers a hundred times more impressions than the artist of the 18th century... The condensing of the modern painting, its variety, and broken forms is the result...
Fernand Léger, 'Current pictorial realisations', *Les Soirées de Paris,* 1914

Apollinaire identified Simultaneity as being part of Picasso's and Braque's attempts through Cubism to represent objects from several angles at once. Though Cubism, with its fragmentation and creation of new 'poetic' truths, had something in common with new interests in the dynamism of modern life, it was also quite different. Futurists and Vorticists denigrated Cubism as being too still, too tasteful, too sterile. Cendrars, Léger and particularly Delaunay struggled against Cubist intellectualism, and looked for an art that was more about life.

What characterises today's style is less noticeable in house or furniture design than in iron constructions, machines, cars, aeroplanes.
Guillaume Apollinaire, 'La Renaissance des Arts décoratifs', 1912

The idea of the vital movements of the world and its movement is simultaneity.
Robert Delaunay, 1912

RAYMOND DUCHAMP-VILLON *Large Horse* 1914

In opposing the simultaneous to the successive, Delaunay launched a whole new way of thinking in the modern arts. Apollinaire named this Orphism, and saw his 'Orphist School' as being about 'an interior vision, more popular, more poetic about the universe and life'. Delaunay was the champion of Apollinaire's school which variously included Sonia Delaunay, Picabia, Duchamp and Léger. The Orphists were as interested as the Futurists in movement. Delaunay quoted Bergson, 'Analytic methods of describing reality cannot grasp mobility which is the essence of the simultaneist consciousness', and Severini explained 'We choose to concentrate our attention on things in motion, because our modern sensibility is particularly qualified to grasp the idea of speed'. However the French criticised the Futurists for using 'cinematic' techniques which broke down speed rather than synthesising it. Though they used different words, the Vorticists also opposed the Futurists' 'dependency' on successivity. The difference between Orphism and Futurism was apparent to the French when they saw the 1912 Futurist exhibition in Paris, though from this date the two groups moved towards a similar approach.

The Delaunays began to use 'simultaneous contrasts' in 1912, and Robert first employed the phrase (borrowed from Chevreul's 1839 book, *De la loi du contraste simultané des couleurs*) in 1913. His work, like that of Sonia, derived as much from Neo-Impressionist colour theories as from ideas of transport and spirituality, but once developed, his simultaneous pictures played an important role in contemporary thinking. This division and re-making of the world was likened to contemporary

ROBERT DELAUNAY *Windows Open Simultaneously (First Part, Third Motif)* 1912

NATALIA GONCHAROVA *Linen* 1913

MIKHAIL LARIONOV *Nocturne* c1913-14

poetry, and has echoes in the poem-conversations written at that time. Severini described Mallarmé's poems thus: 'The words chosen by Mallarmé, according to their complementary quality, employed together or separately, constitute a technique for examining a prismatic subdivision of the idea, a simultaneous co-penetration of images'.

Bergson had written in his *Introduction to Metaphysics*, 'when I speak of an absolute movement, I am attributing to the moving object an inner life, and so to speak, states of mind'. This is close to the role given to 'lines of force' by the Futurists; the lines which they believed 'objects reveal', and which take up the mood of the object, which may be calm or frenzied, sad or gay. The

Futurists intended their lines of force to engage the viewer, and sweep him/her into the picture. The Rayonnism developed in Russia by Mikhail Larionov and Natalia Goncharova has parallels with Futurism both in its pictorial language and, in the case of Goncharova at least, in its subject matter. Whereas Larionov pursued theoretical works, in muted tones, his colleague worked in much brighter colours, and took as her inspiration subjects such as factories, engines and cyclists. However, in terms of the importance to it of painting theory, Rayonnism is closer to Delaunay's Simultaneism, and to the spiritual abstraction developed by the Blaue Reiter.

In 1913 Larionov wrote: 'The style of Rayonnist

MIKHAIL LARIONOV *Rayonnist Drawing* c1911-12   NATALIA GONCHAROVA *Rayonnist Composition* c1912-13

painting promoted by us is concerned with spatial forms which are obtained through the crossing of reflected rays from various objects, and forms which are singled out by the artist. The painting is revealed as a skimmed impression, it is perceived out of time and in space – in it arises the sensation of what could be called the fourth dimension, that is the length, width and thickness of the colour layers. These are the sole symbols of perception which emerge from this painting which is of another order. In this way painting parallels music while remaining itself... Hence the natural downfall of all existing styles and forms in all the art of the past... With this begins the true liberation of painting'.

By 1912 Larionov and Goncharova had begun to reject both their Munich and their Parisian contacts, and had decided to assert the existence of a Russian school. With Malevich and Vladimir Tatlin they organised the *Donkey's Tail* group exhibition. In 1913 Larionov organised a show called *The Target* at which Rayonnism was formally launched. They saw Rayonnism as a synthesis of Cubism, Futurism and Orphism; as a 'style of painting independent of real forms, existing and developing according to the laws of painting'. Futurism continued in various guises in Russia; in the space of 1915 Ivan Puni organised the so-called first *Futurist exhibition: Tramway V* in St Petersburg and then *0:10. The Last Futurist Painting Exhibition.*

C R W NEVINSON *Bursting Shell* 1915

0.10 did indeed sound the death knell for Futurism in its introduction of Malevich's Suprematist paintings. They signified a new stage in the evolution of abstraction.

In 1913 Larionov and Goncharova had declared 'Long live nationality! We are against the West, which is vulgarizing our forms and Eastern forms, and which is bringing down the level of everything'. In this we sense that the internationalism which had been so striking in the prewar period was becoming overlaid with nationalism. In fact internationalism and nationalism had often come hand-in-hand, making uneasy bedfellows, and the very currency of artistic knowledge across Europe had already made for nationalistic rivalry. 'The inspiration of this poem came to me naturally and... has nothing to do with the commercial agitation of M Marinetti', asserted Cendrars in 1913. The French magazine *Nord-Sud* defined Futurism as 'only the artistic appearance of a national Italian awakening. Thus, lots of energy but very little Art'. Marinetti denigrated the Russians with a similarly nationalistic argument: 'the Russians are false Futurists, who distort the true meaning of the great religion for the renewal of the world by means of Futurism'.

Since the Eiffel Tower was built for the Universal Exhibition of 1889 it had enjoyed a second birth. It had come to symbolise the twentieth − rather than the nineteenth − century, and had become a great symbol of international communication. In 1914 its facilities were put to new ends. That August the Tower's receiver picked up a radio message from the German army advancing on Paris. War had arrived, and with it, a new kind of dynamism.

WYNDHAM LEWIS *The Crowd* c1915

THE OLD IN THE NEW

Judith Collins

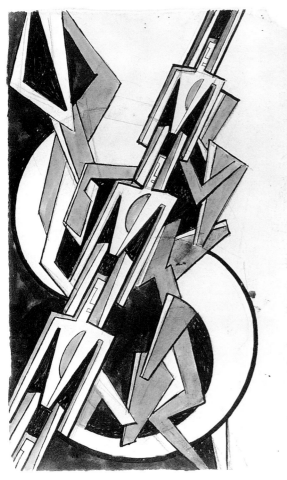

HELEN SAUNDERS *Monochrome Abstract Composition* c1915

This essay seeks to show that although the works of art in this display were created in the heady experimental years of 'Early Modernism', c1910–15, they are steeped in the art of the past. Influences from the art of the past were the dynamic or motivating force behind much that appeared to be new, and the strength of that dynamic assisted in the creation of a new formal language. Artists working in London were clearly affected by voices from the past, perhaps more so than artists in France or Italy. This essay unashamedly concentrates on Britain because there are more works by British artists in the display, and because their works are so rich and innovative.

In London in the two years just prior to the First World War, a handful of artists began to make paintings and drawings of an abstract nature, while a small number of critics and art historians offered encouragement and a sense of direction for their experiments. This essay will attempt to examine the way these artists and critics approached and developed this new abstract style. It will also enquire into the symbiotic relationship between choice of style and choice of subject matter. Young British artists at this time were well informed about contemporary developments in art and literature in France, Italy, Germany and Russia and their abstract works were made to be tested against a European background. Most had spent time in Paris and were informed about the work of the Cubists, while exhibitions of the work of the Italian Futurists were shown in London in 1912–13.

Not all the painters and sculptors who experimented with abstraction in the period 1912-15 subscribed to the movement called Vorticism, but this name is taken as characterising that period. Eight visual artists – Lawrence Atkinson, Henri Gaudier-Brzeska, Jessica Dismorr, Cuthbert Hamilton, William Roberts, Helen Saunders, Edward Wadsworth and Wyndham Lewis – signed the Vorticist Manifesto which was published in the magazine called *Blast*, edited by Wyndham Lewis. This magazine ran to two issues, one published July 1914 and the second in July 1915. The two notable exceptions to this communal signing were David Bomberg and Jacob Epstein. The Vorticist Manifesto does not give an easy explanation of why the work produced by the eight artists looks as it does. The word 'vortex' was purloined by the poet Ezra Pound to describe the new aesthetic aims of this loose grouping of artists: Pound stated that it meant 'the point of maximum energy'.

The poet and critic T E Hulme gave a lecture entitled 'Modern Art and its Philosophy' on 22 January 1914 to the Quest Society, London and the content of his talk was most apposite for both the practical and theoretical needs of his artist colleagues. In the winter of 1912-13 Hulme had travelled to Berlin to talk with the German art historian Wilhelm Worringer, who in 1908 had published a doctoral thesis on the reasons for abstraction in art, with the title *Abstraktion und Einfuhlung* or *Abstraction and Empathy*. Worringer provided psychological reasons for earlier artists' urges towards abstraction and contrasted them with their urges towards realism, or empathy. He believed that abstract art of earlier periods, most particularly Islamic, Byzantine and Celtic, was the product of the artists' obsessional desires to order the world. These desires carried a resonance of the higher divine principle which had caused the world to come into being and had ordered it, and it thus satisfied a deep spiritual need within the artist. Abstract art was therefore not the product of artists with deficient technical ability, who could not create works of mimetic realism. It was instead a particular and deeply felt metaphysical response to the natural world and its objects. Prominent periods of mimetic representation in art could be found in Greek art and the art of the Renaissance. Hulme took on Worringer's views completely and in January 1914 was probably the first person to present them to a London audience. Hulme found that contemporary British representational art, like that of the Greeks and the Renaissance period, was soft and 'sloppy', and not something to be pursued or be proud of in a modern world. He would have known of Bomberg's and Lewis's recent work exemplifying an urge to abstraction and this would

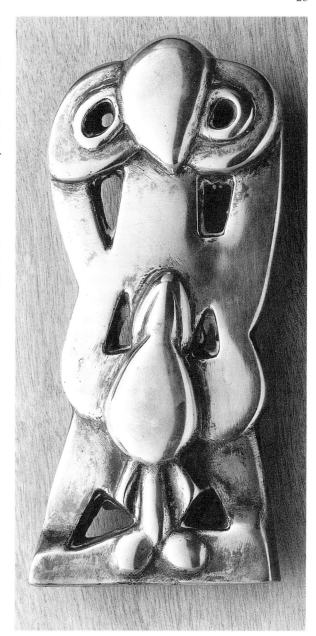

HENRI GAUDIER-BRZESKA *Doorknocker* 1914

HELEN SAUNDERS *Abstract Composition in Blue and Yellow* c1915

WILLIAM ROBERTS *The Diners* 1919

DAVID BOMBERG *Bathing Scene* c1912-13

WYNDHAM LEWIS *Planners: Happy Day* 1912-13

surely have given fuel to his theory.

It has to be remembered that Hulme did not expect his artist colleagues to seek their route to abstraction via the mimetic representation of the most radical mechanical objects of the Edwardian age in which they were living. He was content that they found their desire to simplify from within themselves. Since all were well trained in figurative draughtsmanship and composition by their London art colleges, it was likely that this traditional skill would underlie their more vanguard experimentation. Nor was Hulme happy with art that rejected representation or figuration altogether.

> No artist can create abstract form spontaneously; it is always generated or, at least, suggested, by the consideration of some outside concrete shapes... The interest of the drawing itself depends on the forms it contains. The fact that such forms were suggested by human figures is of no importance.
> (Hulme on William Roberts, *The New Age*, Jan 15 1914)

The abstract work of art had to retain a trace of that which had inspired it, otherwise it would simply be a piece of empty decoration. But the content of the work was to be underplayed in favour of the forms used, except that, as Hulme wrote, abstract or pure forms had to convey 'the ordinary everyday human emotions' by a process in which 'form becomes the porter or carrier of internal emotions'. Hulme tended to play down the subject of a work, as can be seen from his quote about Roberts above, yet in contrast the young artists that he admired were persistent in giving the majority of their avant-garde abstract drawings and paintings strong literary or allegorical titles. The significance of these titles has been somewhat neglected and this essay is in part an attempt to redress that balance.

For the painters Lewis, Bomberg and Roberts, and Epstein the sculptor, the original inspiration was always the human figure. The painters paid particular interest to the theme of movement, characterised by the human figure caught in physical action. They shared an interest in dancers, acrobats, the theatre and the circus. They often chose to present performers on a stage, albeit in abstracted form, playing their part in the creation of an illusion for the viewer. If the Futurists in Italy glorified the sleek lines of a metal machine, the British artists in contrast admired the efficiency of a well-exercised human body under conscious mental control. There was an almost total disregard for the still life as subject matter. Wyndham Lewis wrote about Picasso's cubist collages and constructions of c1913-14, disparagingly describing

WILLIAM ROBERTS *The Return of Ulysses* 1913

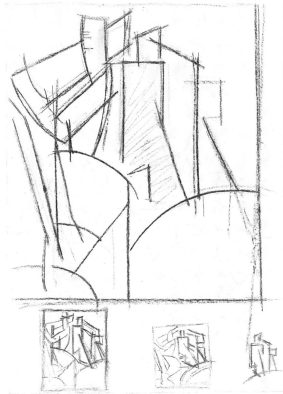

DAVID BOMBERG *Sketches for 'The Dancer'* c1913-14

C R W NEVINSON *The Arrival* 1923-24

CUTHBERT HAMILTON *Reconstruction* 1919-20

WYNDHAM LEWIS *Two Mechanics* c1912

them as 'little Nature-mortes… a sort of new little parasite bred on machinery'. He felt that the Cubists' concentration on the genre of the still-life meant that they lacked a sense of seriousness in their approach to their art. No doubt the other English artists would have concurred with him in that opinion.

Wyndham Lewis's pen and ink drawings of 1912-13 depict nude figures, mostly male, in barren landscapes, with only an odd tree decorating the horizon. The figures are rarely alone, and from their titles, such as 'Courtship' and 'Ritualistic Challenge', it can be inferred that they are occupied in physical and psychological attitudes and confrontations. Much is made of their developed musculature and the significance of their gestures. Lewis stated that 'Buonarroti is my bête-noir' and it is obvious that Michelangelo's heroic nudes have had some influence here. Michelangelo's contorted nude male figures, the 'ignudi' on the Sistine Chapel ceiling, led in the latter half of the sixteenth century to the movement known as Mannerism, which is characterised by sensuous figures caught in contorted and complex dynamics, usually painted in sharp, acid colours, with strong attention given to their outlines. Perhaps Lewis's Vorticist phase can be seen as the last outburst of Mannerism.

Lewis's ink and watercolour drawing 'Two Mechanics', c1912, consists of two naked muscular men striding to the left while turning their heads to look out at the viewer. They clamp their hands together in their genital regions, rather like the pose defensive footballers adopt when standing in the wall waiting before a penalty kick. The word 'mechanic' can mean a man 'acting in the manner of a machine' and Lewis could well have wished to draw attention to this aspect of humankind, possibly implying that this kind of man was predominantly governed by the mechanical impulses of his loins. This drawing also stands in an interesting relationship with Jacob Epstein's c1913 drawings for his sculpture 'The Rock Drill'.

Besides Michelangelo who dogged Lewis's drawings and paintings, there was also Shakespeare and Elizabethan drama that influenced Lewis's writings. Lewis placed 'Shakespeare' in the Bless section of the Vorticist Manifesto, 'for his bitter

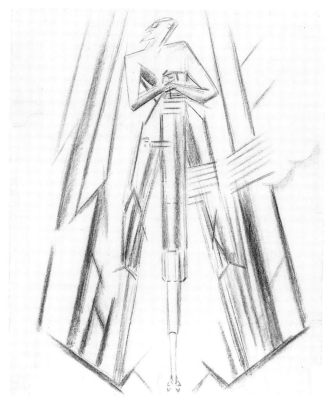

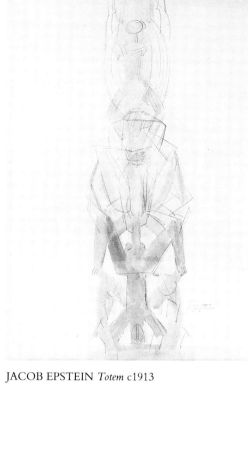

JACOB EPSTEIN *Study for 'The Rock Drill'* c1913

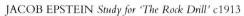

JACOB EPSTEIN *Totem* c1913

Northern Rhetoric of humour'. Shakespeare was a Northener and far superior, implied Lewis, to Southerners who suffer from Romanticism, such as the Futurists. The English 'are the inventors of this bareness and hardness, and should be the great enemies of Romance... The Latins are at present ... in their "discovery" of sport, their Futurist gush over machines, aeroplanes, etc., the most romantic and sentimental "moderns" to be found'. Lewis was not afraid of stating his influences from the past and then reviving them. The Italian Futurists, by contrast, proclaimed in their manifestos that the past had to be destroyed. One of the aims of Vorticism was 'to establish what we consider to be characteristic in the consciousness and form content of our time: then to dig to the durable simplicity by which that can be most grandly and distinctly expressed'. Undoubtedly the 'consciousness and form content' of Lewis and his colleagues' work was affected by the time in which they lived: a world full of rapid changes and increased speed in communication, for example electricity and

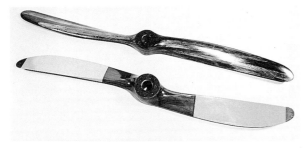

First World War aircraft propellers

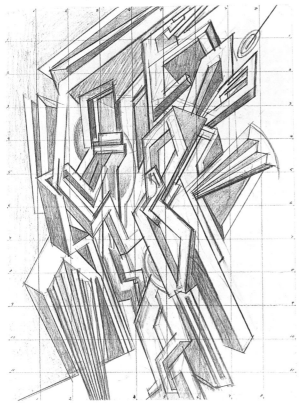

WILLIAM ROBERTS *Study for 'Two Step'* 1915

telephones, new forms of travel plus the looming spectre of major conflict. Nevinson's 'The Arrival' is a good example of a painting that tries to capture some of this, with its faceted composition with shifting viewpoints. But since the form was to be expressive of an inner, emotional content, as proposed by Hulme, it was surely less easy to express the inner nature of a transatlantic liner, as in the Nevinson, than to express the inner nature of a man and woman dancing together, as in Roberts's 'The Two-Step'.

Besides Hulme, the other critics in London who assisted in the development of a new style were the duo of Roger Fry and Clive Bell, promoters of significant form, and Laurence Binyon, poet and art historian, who took charge of the oriental prints and drawings department at the British Museum in 1913. By that date he had already written *Painting in the Far East*, in 1908 and *The Flight of the Dragon*, a book 'on the theory and practice of art in China and Japan', in 1911. Binyon was largely responsible for fostering an interest in the rhythms of a composition. In the first chapter of *The Flight of the Dragon*, he set forth the six canons which form the fundamental principles of Chinese art, laid down in the sixth century. After reminding the reader that exact translation is impossible, he gave the primary canon as 'Rhythmic Vitality, or Spiritual Rhythm expressed in the movement of life', and continued: 'what is meant is that the artist must pierce beneath the mere aspect of the world to seize and himself be possessed by that great cosmic rhythm of the spirit which sets the currents of life in motion' (p 13). The rhythm is that of man and his spirit, not that of the machine. When Binyon attempted to define rhythm a couple of pages later he wrote: 'we are probably nearer to its essence when we speak of the rhythmical movements of the body, as in games or the dance'. After conceding that works of art are in a different category from that of sport or ballet, Binyon continued:

> Sculpture and painting are not, it is true, capable of actual movement, but they suggest movement. Every statue, every picture, is a series of ordered relations, controlled, as the body is controlled in the dance, by the will to express a single idea. A study of the most

DAVID BOMBERG *Vision of Ezekiel* 1912

rudimentary abstract design will show that the units of line or mass are in reality energies capable of acting on each other; and, if we discover a way to put these energies into rhythmical relation, the design at once becomes animated, our imagination enters into it; our minds also are brought into rhythmical relation with the design, which has become charged with the capability of movement and of life. (pp 17-18)

Bomberg produced a group of paintings of animated figural groups during the years 1912-14, the most astonishing being 'The Vision of Ezekiel',

1912, 'In the Hold', 1913-14 and 'The Mud Bath', 1914, the first of which was painted while he was still a student at the Slade School. His teacher of drawing at the Slade, Henry Tonks, used to uphold the tradition of academic draughtsmanship by asking his students to plot the form of the live model 'from point to point'. Bomberg, with a brave independence, indicated that he felt this process, although resulting in accuracy, lacked depth and a sense of the presence of mass. Possibly his deep admiration for Michelangelo led him to conceive of forms derived from the human figure as compact masses, stripped of detail and made up from simplified directional planes. When Bomberg

DAVID BOMBERG *In the Hold* c1913-14

laid a divisional grid over the animated figures in 'Ju-Jitsu', and 'In the Hold', he was emphasising the directional rhythms and energies of the masses, and charging them with 'the capability of movement and of life'.

The Slade School encouraged monthly competitions in imaginative pictorial design, for which much preparatory drawing was necessary. The way to transfer a working drawing on to a canvas was to square it up, laying a grid of horizontal, vertical and diagonal pencil lines both over the finished drawing and on to the bare canvas. The marks made in each segment of the grid on the drawing could then be translated into the relevant segment of the grid on the canvas. As

the painting was executed on the canvas, the pencil grid was gradually obliterated by coloured pigment, although it can often be glimpsed in paintings by Sickert, for example. Bomberg dared to keep that grid not only visible, but make it the dominant motif in the painting. A chequerboard grid was a compositional device favoured by some contemporary artists working in Paris, for example Juan Gris, Jean Metzinger and Marc Chagall and it has been suggested that they used it to allude to the fourth dimension. The fourth dimension takes one beyond the three other measureable dimensions of line, surface and mass into a more cosmic frame of reference, that of time. Although Bomberg could well have known of the use of the chequerboard in

DAVID BOMBERG *Study for 'The Vision of Ezekiel'* 1912

Parisian art works, it is not known whether he wished to exploit its relationship with the fourth dimension.

From 1910 to 1914 there was a strong thread in Bomberg's subject material of what can be classified as his Jewish heritage. A high proportion of paintings and drawings from these years bear Old Testament titles, for example 'Judgement of Solomon', 'Job and his Comforters', 'Garden of Eden', 'Ruth lieth at Boaz's feet', 'Jereboam', 'Adam and God', 'The Lamentations of Jeremiah', 'The Song of Songs', the series of 'Vision of Ezekiel' works, 'Chinnereth', 'Study for Reading from the Torah' and 'Zin'. A large number of these works were included in Bomberg's first one-man

exhibition at the Chenil Gallery, London, in July 1914. Bomberg's foreword to his Chenil Gallery catalogue contained the oft-quoted statement: 'I look upon Nature, while I live in a steel city'. For an artist who professed to look on nature while acknowledging that his surroundings were hard and inflexible, it is obvious that his head and his heart were also very full of heroic, prophetic figures from the Bible.

The subject matter of 'The Mud Bath' was taken from Jewish daily life in the East End of London, where Bomberg and his family grew up. There was a 'Russian Vapour Baths', founded by a Russian Jewish immigrant, the Reverend B Schevzik. It was situated in Brick Lane, directly opposite the

DAVID BOMBERG *The Mud Bath* 1914

oldest Jewish synagogue in the East End, the Spitalfields Great Synagogue. The customs of the orthodox Jewish religion required the bathing in a ritual bath every Friday evening before the Sabbath commenced, and on other special holy times of the year. Although the painting is stark and pared down to its essence in the presentation of forms and colours, it is full of emotive meaning for the artist. It presents ritual actions as a preparation for abstinence. It is the embodiment of Binyon's 'Spiritual Rhythm expressed in the movement of life'.

ART, ACTION AND THE MACHINE
Paul O'Keeffe

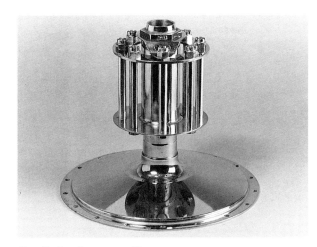

Propeller boss for First World War rotary aircraft engine

A racing car whose hood is adorned with great pipes, like serpents of explosive breath – a roaring car that seems to ride on grapeshot is more beautiful than the 'Victory of Samothrace'.[1]
The Foundation and Manifesto of Futurism, 1909

Nine years into the twentieth century the headless winged figure which towers over visitors on the grand staircase of the Louvre, an age-old aesthetic ideal, was formally declared defunct. Orders were sent out to set fire to library shelves, demolish academies and divert the canals of Venice to flood the museums – a holocaust of burning books, smashed statues, and shredded canvases swept away amongst the wreckage of blazing gondolas by a torrent of filthy water. The author of this apocalyptic vision, F T Marinetti, was the poet of a brave new technological world. In place of what he called *passéism,* the enfeebled established order of 'old masters', he established *Futurism,* a machine age aesthetic which drew its inspiration from everything that was powerful and 'new': electricity, locomotives, aeroplanes and the internal combustion engine. Supplanting a celebrated classical sculpture by a Bugatti heralded this shift in aesthetic preoccupation.

Futurism was launched in Milan with a plethora of manifestos written by Marinetti and the artists under his sway: Giacomo Balla, Umberto Boccioni, Carlo Carrà, Luigi Russolo and Gino Severini. A childlike enthusiasm for the 'new' was invariably couched in the most purple of prose:

…the triumphant progress of science makes profound changes in humanity inevitable, changes which are hacking an abyss between those docile slaves of past tradition and us free moderns, who are confident in the radiant splendour of our future…Living art draws its life from the surrounding environment…we must breathe in the tangible miracles of contemporary life – the iron network of speedy communi-

UMBERTO BOCCIONI
Unique Forms of Continuity in Space 1913

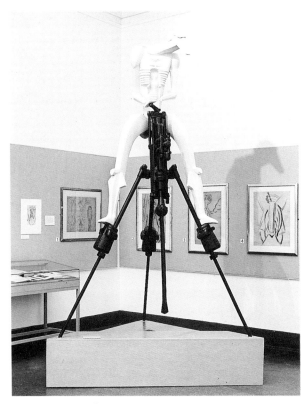

Reconstruction of Epstein's *Rock Drill*

WYNDHAM LEWIS *Composition* 1913

cations which envelops the earth, the transatlantic liners, the dreadnoughts, those marvellous flights which furrow our skies, the profound courage of our submarine navigators and the spasmodic struggle to conquer the unknown.[2]

Marinetti toured Europe with his Futurist colleagues spreading the new art gospel. He had a positive genius for publicity. Wherever he went he published articles and manifestos, gave lectures and declaimed noisy, onomatopoeic Futurist poetry, of which *Zang Tumb Tuuum,* an account of the military bombardment at the siege of Adrianople, was the most notorious example. In 1910 he made the first of several visits to England.

In London as elsewhere, before the Great War, an interest in machinery prevailed among avant-garde artists. Jacob Epstein mounted a plaster sculpture of a robot-like figure on a huge second-hand pneumatic drill previously used for quarrying rock. Wyndham Lewis praised the ports of Hull, Liverpool, London, Newcastle-on-Tyne, Bristol and Glasgow for their 'heavy insect dredgers/ monotonous cranes/lighthouses, blazing through the frosty starlight, cutting the storm like a cake'.[3] Epstein's champion, the critic and poet T E Hulme, signalled the direction twentieth century art was taking:

> There is a desire among modern artists to avoid those lines and surfaces which look pleasing and organic, and to use lines which are clean, clear-cut and mechanical. You will find artists expressing admiration for engineers' drawings, where the lines are clean, the curves all geometrical, and the colour, laid on to show the shape of a cylinder for example, gradated absolutely mechanically. You will find a sculptor disliking the pleasing kind of patina that comes in time on an old bronze and expressing admiration for the hard clean surface of a piston rod.[4]

Hulme's statement pointed to an important distinction between the work of the Futurists, who took their subject matter from modern technology, and those English artists, like Lewis, who eschewed

GIACOMO BALLA *Abstract Speed – the Car has passed* 1913

such representation in favour of a form of abstraction which owed its very style to the characteristics of machinery: hard-edged precision, spareness and efficiency. It was a distinction between form and content.

Although the inspiration and subject matter of Futurist art was indisputably up to date, the style used to produce it recalled an earlier school, expressive of atmospherics and the fleeting moment: Impressionism. The late nineteenth century French painters produced impressions of a foggy harbour or trees in a heat-haze by blurring the outlines of things. Although such subjects were invariably static, the Futurists, who worshipped speed as one of the primary characteristics of the machine age, used a similar lack of linear definition to create the impression of a moving automobile,

locomotive or aeroplane: a blur of wheels, pistons or propellers. If Claude Monet had painted a high powered speed boat scything through the water lilies at Giverny, he would have been a proto-Futurist. It is an outlandish concept of this kind that springs to mind from Ezra Pound's dismissal of the Italian movement as 'an accelerated sort of Impressionism'.[5]

Another stylistic trait owed a great deal to the experiments with multi-exposure photography conducted by Muybridge and Marey in the 1870s and '80s. The repetition and superimposition of images gave the impression of movement, so that, according to one Futurist manifesto: 'a running horse has not four legs, but twenty, and their movements are triangular'.[6] Balla painted a little girl running along a balcony, her head and legs

WYNDHAM LEWIS *Vorticist Composition* 1915

serialized from right to left of the canvas against a row of railings. In 'Dynamism of a dog on a leash', a blurred succession of feet walk a centipedal dachshund. The concept of objective reality was rejected in favour of a world of miracles. To the subjective eye, when a man sat down, his body penetrated the chair and the chair penetrated his body. A horse at the end of the street passed through a face. The same street, wet with rain, formed a mirror in which walls of the buildings on either side plunged deep into the earth. 'Thousands of miles divide us from the sun; yet the house in front of us fits into the solar disc'.[7]

The following dialogue occurred in a London toilet while Marinetti was sluicing himself down with cold water after giving a particularly strenuous public lecture:

Marinetti: Have you ever travelled at a kilometre a minute?
Lewis: Never. I loathe anything that goes too quickly. If it goes too quickly, it is not there.
Marinetti: It is not there! It is *only* when it goes quickly that it *is* there!
Lewis: That is nonsense. I cannot see a thing that is going too quickly.
Marinetti: See it – see it! Why should you want to *see?* But you *do* see it. You see it multiplied a thousand times. You see a thousand things instead of one thing.
Lewis: That's just what I don't want to see. I prefer *one* thing.
Marinetti: There is no such thing as *one* thing.
Lewis: There is if I wish to have it so. And I wish to have it so.
Marinetti: You are a monist!
Lewis: All right. I am not a futurist anyway. *Je hais le mouvement qui déplace les lignes.*[8]

'I hate movement that blurs the lines'. Lewis's riposte exposed the aesthetic and stylistic gulf between Futurism and the London avant-garde. The sharply defined, crystalline abstractions produced by painters like David Bomberg, William Roberts, Edward Wadsworth and Lewis himself had little in common with the frenetic Italian expressions of speed and violence. At the time his conversation with Marinetti occurred Lewis's rival

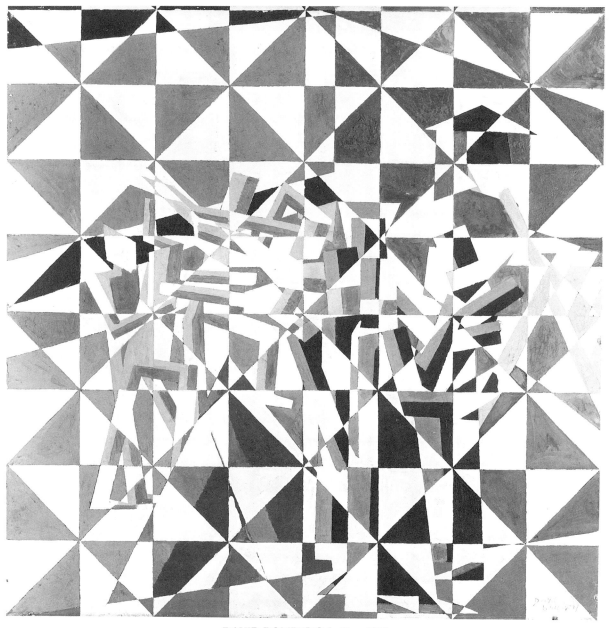

DAVID BOMBERG *Ju-Jitsu* c1913

movement did not have a name. In 1914 Ezra Pound called it not Monism but Vorticism.

The American poet saw in Lewis's work 'every kind of whirlwind of force and emotion. Vortex'.[9] The term was not intended to have any of the Futurist connotations of whirling, violent speed. Implicit in Pound's concept of a vortex was a paradoxical stillness: the 'stillness' and stability of a rapidly spinning top. Lewis explained it as follows:

You think at once of a whirlpool. At the heart of the whirlpool is a great silent place where all the energy is concentrated. And there at the point of concentration is the Vorticist.[10]

Futurism on the other hand was, according to Pound: 'the disgorging spray of a vortex with no drive behind it, DISPERSAL'.[11] Such distinctions might sound a little trivial today but it should be

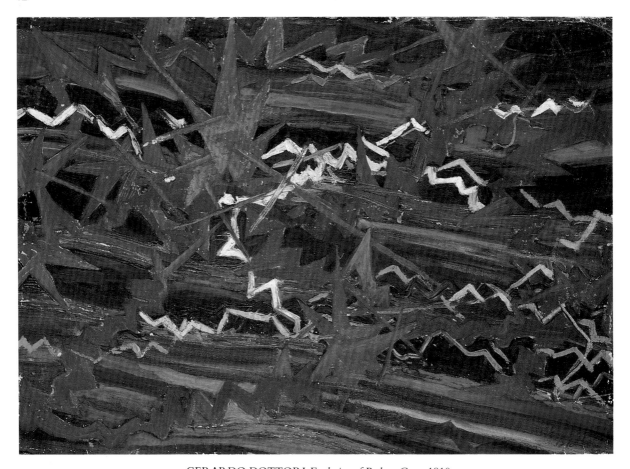

GERARDO DOTTORI *Explosion of Red on Green* 1910

WYNDHAM LEWIS *Workshop* c1914–15

LAWRENCE ATKINSON *The Lake* c1915-20

JESSICA DISMORR *Abstract Composition* c1915

HELEN SAUNDERS *Abstract Multicoloured Design* c1915

remembered that this was a period of high profile art politics when the squabbles between rival factions of painters were regularly reported in the national press. In the summer of 1914 such disputes seemed important. 'Life was one big bloodless brawl, prior to the Great Bloodletting',[12] as Lewis recalled later.

Marinetti had come to London looking for recruits. But only one English painter broke ranks and aligned himself with Futurism. C R W Nevinson had been a close friend and colleague of Lewis and had, along with Lawrence Atkinson, Gaudier-Brzeska, Jessica Dismorr, Cuthbert Hamilton, Helen Saunders, Roberts, Wadsworth and Pound, helped to set up Vorticist headquarters in Great Ormond Street: the Rebel Art Centre. He it was who suggested the explosive title *Blast* for the gigantic puce-coloured journal that Lewis edited and largely filled with his own contributions. Following his defection to the Futurist camp, Nevinson appended his name to one of Marinetti's manifestos printed in *The Observer, The Times* and *Daily Mail,* giving his address as The Rebel Art Centre. Lewis and his colleagues in Great Ormond Street felt themselves to be seriously compromised by the gesture and it was this which provoked the outbreak of hostilities between the two gangs. Marinetti's flair for publicity had made him a household name and every work of art that departed even slightly from the representational norm was dubbed 'futurist' by press and public alike. In order that a fledgling English movement could flourish in its own right, rather than be seen as an adjunct to Futurism, it was necessary to differentiate itself entirely. The most effective means of differentiation was antagonism. It was, as Lewis said, a 'bloodless brawl' and the nearest it came to physical violence was when a group of Vorticists arrived at the Doré Gallery to barrack one of Marinetti's lectures. Hostilities were more usually engaged in on the field of journalism.

It was a clash between North and South, between Latin and Anglo-Saxon and a major divergence was to be found in the rival groups' attitude to machinery. This was highlighted by Lewis with a certain degree of national pride spiked with attendant xenophobia:

> …England practically invented this civilisation that Signor Marinetti has come to preach to us about. While Italy was still a Borgia-haunted swamp of intrigue, England was buckling on the brilliant and electric armour of the modern world, and sending out her inventions and new spirit across Europe and America. That in the year 1914 a Milanese should suddenly arrive on these shores and overwhelm us with his contempt and objurations because we are supposed by him not to appreciate motor-cars is absurd…[13]

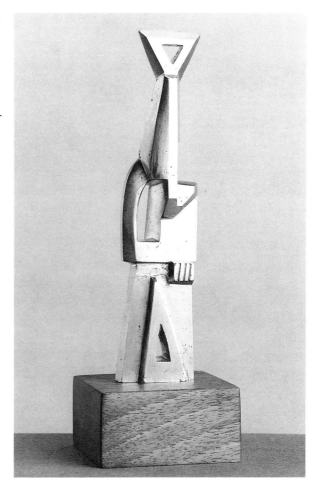

HENRI GAUDIER-BRZESKA *Ornament* 1914

Or as he more succinctly put it, in conversation, to Marinetti himself: 'You Wops insist too much on the Machine. You're always on about these driving-belts, you are always exploding about internal combustion. We've had machines here in England for a donkey's years. They're no novelty to us'.[14] It would have come as an unbearable affront to the messiah of the 'new' to be accused of being *passéist*.

Another charge levelled against Futurism would have been equally insulting to Marinetti: that it was, despite its manifestos against the Past, the Tango and *Parsifal,* inherently romantic. It was even linked retrospectively with the execrable 'mauve Nineties', as Lewis reminded his readers: 'Wilde gushed twenty years ago about the beauty of machinery'.[15] Indeed, the very enthusiasm with which the latin temperament embraced the

wonders of the modern world was, to the cool classical mind, characteristically romantic. T E Hulme, a self-proclaimed classicist, believed 'that after a hundred years of romanticism we are in for a classical revival'.[16] In the vanguard of this revival he placed the stark geometrical precision of paintings by Lewis and Bomberg, the cold smooth surfaces of an Epstein or a Gaudier-Brzeska sculpture. Compared to this formal clarity, the blurred lines which characterised the Futurist deification of flux was anathema. Expression of movement in the static media of painting and sculpture was heretical to the classical sensibility because it symbolically broke down barriers which alone maintained order and stability in the world. Hulme's view of romanticism was a state in which 'concepts that are right and proper in their own sphere are spread over, and so mess up, falsify and blur the outlines of human experience. It is like pouring a pot of treacle over the dinner table'.[17] Pound's theory of art also insisted on rigidly defined compartments:

> Every concept…presents itself to the vivid consciousness in some primary form. It belongs to the art of this form. If sound, to music; if formed words, to literature; the image, to poetry; form, to design; colour in position, to painting; form or design in three planes, to sculpture; movement to the dance or to the rhythm of music or of verses.[18]

It should not be assumed however that the English avant-garde, although largely in agreement on matters of aesthetics and united against the Futurist interlopers, formed a wholly integrated group. Jacob Epstein declined to identify himself with the Rebel Art Centre. He nevertheless allowed two of his drawings to appear in *Blast*. The fiercely individualistic David Bomberg refused to concede even that much to group activity and threatened to sue Lewis if he reproduced any of his work. Pound irritated Hulme who was only waiting for an excuse to kick the poet downstairs. Hulme and Lewis, despite having a great many philosophical ideas in common, eventually severed relations with a fist-fight over a woman, which culminated in Lewis being left suspended upside down by his trouser turn-ups on the railings of Soho Square.

When that long hot summer of 1914 ended with a spark in Sarajevo that ignited the four-year conflagration of World War, the combative politics of art, together with more personal antagonisms, paled into insignificance. The following year, in the second and last issue of *Blast*, the 'War Number', Lewis admitted that things had changed and his enterprise was hopelessly upstaged by events: '*Blast* finds itself surrounded by a multitude of other Blasts of all sizes and descriptions'.[19]

Back in Milan, the Futurists were overjoyed as the conflict spread across Europe towards neutral Italy. They set up a persistent clamour of manifestos and demonstrations. They burned Austrian flags and wore 'anti-neutralist clothes', an invention of Balla. Marinetti is said to have distributed hand grenades to his friends. War embodied all the Futurist ideals of violent action and the triumph of

German First World War rifle-grenade throwing rest

C R W NEVINSON *Bursting Shell* 1915

C R W NEVINSON *Study for 'Returning to the Trenches'* 1914-15

modern technology. When Italy entered hostilities, the Futurists enlisted en masse. Boccioni was killed, together with the brilliant Futurist architect Antonio Sant'Elia.

In London, Nevinson told the *Daily Express:* 'This war will be a violent incentive to Futurism, for we believe there is no beauty except in strife, no masterpiece without aggressiveness'.[20] Found unfit for active service, he joined the Red Cross and went to France as an ambulance driver. Lewis trained as a gunner and commanded a howitzer battery at the battle of Passchendaele. Bomberg, Roberts and Wadsworth went into uniform, as did Hulme who was blown to pieces by a direct hit half-a-mile along the line from Lewis's battery. Gaudier-Brzeska was killed in a charge at Neuville St Vaast; the announcement of his death appeared, edged in black, in the last issue of *Blast*.

The mechanical holocaust of the First World War decimated a generation. It also forced artists and intellectuals to confront their theories with practice, their ideas about modern technology with the reality of its products: barbed wire, mustard gas, the tank, the machine gun and the high explosive artillery bombardment. Nevinson's work, in particular, underwent a startling change between 1914 and 1918. His prewar style was ideally suited, initially, to the portrayal of modern warfare; the facetted, interpenetrating forms of a column of French soldiers, 'Returning to the Front', merged individuals into a corporate mass, a fighting machine. By 1918 he had abandoned Futurist dynamics in favour of a more realistic style partly from disgust with the war and partly as a result of the documentary obligation imposed upon him by his work as an official war artist. These two impulses towards realism were not always compatible; his ironically titled 'Paths of Glory', showing two dead English soldiers on the parapet of a trench, had to be censored on the grounds that only realistic impressions of German corpses could be officially countenanced by the military authorities.

The archetypal product of machine age art was Epstein's 'The Rock Drill'. It was begun in 1913 in an innocent spirit of enthusiasm for machinery. It was exhibited in 1915 when an innocence still prevailed in London about the war raging on the other side of the Channel. In the horrific year of 1916, when innocence was lost and modern war came of age on the battlefield of the Somme, Epstein's enthusiasm for machinery evaporated. He discarded the drill. He hacked off the right arm of the plaster figure, together with the buttocks and legs, and cast the torso. Emasculated, mutilated and defeated in permanent bronze, it stands as an awesome monument to Experience.

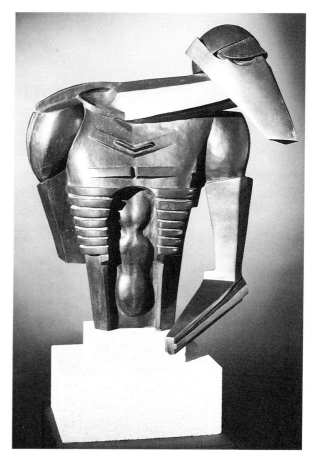

JACOB EPSTEIN *Torso in Metal from 'The Rock Drill'* 1913
(not in exhibition)

NOTES

1 F T Marinetti, 'The Founding and Manifesto of Futurism', 1909, reprinted, *Futurist Manifestos* (ed. U Apollonio), London, 1973, p 21.

2 Umberto Boccioni, et al, 'Manifesto of the Futurist Painters', 1910, reprinted, *Futurist Manifestos*, pp 24-25.

3 Wyndham Lewis, *Blast*, London, 1914, p 23.

4 T E Hulme, *Speculations* (ed. H Read), London, 1924, p 97.

5 Ezra Pound, 'Vortex, Pound', *Blast*, 1914, p 154.

6 Umberto Boccioni, et al, 'Futurist Painting: Technical Manifesto', 1910, reprinted, *Futurist Manifestos*, p 28.

7 *Ibid.*

8 See Wyndham Lewis, *Blasting and Bombardiering,* London, 1937, p 38.

9 Ezra Pound, *Letters* (ed. D D Paige), London, 1951, p 122.

10 See Douglas Goldring, *South Lodge,* London, 1943, p 65.

11 Ezra Pound, 'Vortex, Pound', *Blast,* 1914, p 153.

12 Wyndham Lewis, *Blasting and Bombardiering,* p 39.

13 Wyndham Lewis, 'Automobilism', 1914, reprinted, *Creatures of Habit and Creatures of Change* (ed. P Edwards) Santa Rosa, 1989, pp 33-34.

14 Wyndham Lewis, *Blasting and Bombardiering,* p 37.

15 Wyndham Lewis, *Blast,* 1914, p [8].

16 T E Hulme, *Speculations,* p 113.

17 T E Hulme, *Speculations,* p 118.

18 Ezra Pound, 'Vortex, Pound', *Blast,* 1914, p 154.

19 Wyndham Lewis, *Blast* no 2, London, 1915, p 5.

20 Quoted in William C Wees, *Vorticism and the English Avant-Garde,* Manchester, 1972, p 118.

LIST OF WORKS IN THE DISPLAY

Dimensions: height followed by width (followed by depth) in millimetres.

Identification numbers are those of the Tate Gallery catalogue.

Page numbers refer to illustrations of the works.

LAWRENCE ATKINSON 1873-1931
The Lake
c1915-20
Watercolour on paper
254 x 368
T00717 (p 44)

GIACOMO BALLA 1871-1958
Abstract Speed – the Car has passed
Velocità astratta – L'Auto è passata
1913
Oil on canvas
502 x 654
T01222 (p 39)

UMBERTO BOCCIONI 1882-1916
Unique Forms of Continuity in Space
Forme uniche della continuità nello spazio
1913
Bronze
1175 x 876 x 368
T01589 (p 37)

DAVID BOMBERG 1890-1957
Ju-Jitsu
c1913
Oil on board
619 x 619
T00585 (p 41)

DAVID BOMBERG 1890-1957
The Mud Bath
1914
Oil on canvas
1524 x 2242
T00656 (p 36)

DAVID BOMBERG 1890-1957
In the Hold
c1913-14
Oil on canvas
1962 x 2311
T00913 (p 34)

DAVID BOMBERG 1890-1957
Bathing Scene
c1912-13
Oil on panel
559 x 686
T01055 (p 26)

DAVID BOMBERG 1890-1957
Vision of Ezekiel
1912
Oil on canvas
1143 x 1372
T01197 (p 33)

DAVID BOMBERG 1890-1957
Study for 'The Vision of Ezekiel'
1912
Charcoal and pencil on paper
565 x 686
T01681 (p 35)

DAVID BOMBERG 1890-1957
Sketches for 'The Dancer'
c1913-14
Charcoal on paper
381 x 279
T01961 (p 27)

ROBERT DELAUNAY 1885-1941
Windows Open Simultaneously (First Part, Third Motif)
Fenêtres ouvertes simultanément (1ère Partie, 3me Motif)
1912
Oil on canvas
457 x 375
T00920 (p 16)

SONIA DELAUNAY 1885-1979
Prose of the Trans-Siberian Railway and of Little Jehanne of France
La prose du Transsibérien et de la Petite Jehanne de France
1913
Gouache stencil print
1956 x 356
P07355 (p 11)

JESSICA DISMORR 1885-1939
Abstract Composition
c1915
Oil on composition board
413 x 508
T01084 (p 44)

GERARDO DOTTORI 1884-1977
Explosion of Red on Green
Esplosione di rosso sul verde
1910
Oil on canvas
492 x 695
T01336 (p 42)

RAYMOND DUCHAMP-VILLON
1876-1918
Large Horse
Le Grand Cheval
1914
Bronze
1000 x 987 x 660
T02307 (p 15)

JACOB EPSTEIN 1880-1959
Study for 'The Rock Drill'
c 1913
Charcoal on paper
641 x 533
T00363 (p 31)

JACOB EPSTEIN 1880-1959
Totem
c 1913
Pencil and watercolour on paper
580 x 415
T03358 (p 31)

NAUM GABO 1890-1977
Kinetic Sculpture (Standing Wave)
(1920/1985)
Metal rod with electric motor
616 x 241 x 190
T00827 (right)

HENRI GAUDIER-BRZESKA
1891-1915
Doorknocker
1914
Polished bronze
171 x 79 x 29
T00841 (p 23)

HENRI GAUDIER-BRZESKA
1891-1915
Ornament
1914
Bronze
156 x 38 x 32
T01097 (p 45)

ALBERT GLEIZES 1881-1953
Portrait of Jacques Nayral
1911
Oil on canvas
1619 x 1140
T02410 (p 8)

NATALIA GONCHAROVA
1881-1962
Linen
1913
Oil on canvas
956 x 838
N06194 (p 17)

NATALIA GONCHAROVA
1881-1962
Rayonnist Composition
c 1912-13
Pastel on paper
318 x 216
T01119 (p 19)

CUTHBERT HAMILTON 1885-1959
Reconstruction
1919-20
Ink and gouache on paper
559 x 419
T00758 (p 29)

MIKHAIL LARIONOV 1881-1964
Nocturne
c 1913-14
Oil on canvas
502 x 610
N06192 (p 18)

MIKHAIL LARIONOV 1881-1964
Rayonnist Drawing
c 1911-12
Charcoal on paper
241 x 159
T01325 (p 19)

WYNDHAM LEWIS 1882-1957
Composition
1913
Watercolour, ink and pencil on paper
343 x 267
N05886 (p 38)

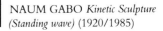

NAUM GABO *Kinetic Sculpture
(Standing wave)* (1920/1985)

WYNDHAM LEWIS 1882-1957
The Crowd
?exhibited 1915
Oil on canvas
2007 x 1537
T00689 (p 21)

WYNDHAM LEWIS 1882-1957
Workshop
c1914-15
Oil on canvas
765 x 610
T01931 (p 43)

WYNDHAM LEWIS 1882-1957
Vorticist Composition
1915
Gouache and black chalk on paper
314 x 178
T00625 (p 40)

WYNDHAM LEWIS 1882-1957
Planners: Happy Day
1912-13
Ink, pencil and gouache on paper
311 x 381
T00106 (p 26)

WYNDHAM LEWIS 1882-1957
Two Mechanics
c1912
Ink and wash on paper
559 x 337
T00108 (p 30)

JOHN MARIN 1870-1953
Downtown, New York
1923
Watercolour on paper
679 x 552
T00080 (p 7)

CHRISTOPHER RICHARD
WYNNE NEVINSON 1889-1946
The Arrival
1923-24
Oil on canvas
762 x 635
T00110 (pp 12,28)

CHRISTOPHER RICHARD
WYNNE NEVINSON 1889-1946
Study for 'Returning to the Trenches'
1914-15
Ink on paper
146 x 206
T00249 (p 48)

CHRISTOPHER RICHARD
WYNNE NEVINSON 1889-1946
Dance Hall Scene
c1913-14
Gouache and ink on paper
222 x 197
T01913 (front cover, p 7)

CHRISTOPHER RICHARD
WYNNE NEVINSON 1889-1946
Bursting Shell
1915
Oil on canvas
760 x 560
T03676 (pp 20,47)

WILLIAM ROBERTS 1895-1980
The Return of Ulysses
1913
Ink on paper
305 x 457
T00878 (p 27)

WILLIAM ROBERTS 1895-1980
Study for 'Two Step'
1915
Drawing on paper
298 x 229
T01100 (p 32)

WILLIAM ROBERTS 1895-1980
The Diners
1919
Oil on canvas
1524 x 832
T00230 (p 25)

HELEN SAUNDERS 1885-1963
Monochrome Abstract Composition
c1915
Ink and wash over pencil
289 x 184
T00622 (p 22)

HELEN SAUNDERS 1885-1963
Abstract Composition in Blue and Yellow
c1915
Watercolour on paper
276 x 171
T00623 (p 24)

HELEN SAUNDERS 1885-1963
Abstract Multicoloured Design
c1915
Ink and gouache on paper
359 x 257
T00624 (p 44)

GINO SEVERINI 1883-1966
Suburban Train Arriving in Paris
Train de Banlieue arrivant à Paris
1915
Oil on canvas
886 x 1156
T01070 (p 13)

EDWARD WADSWORTH 1889-1949
View of a Town
c1918
Woodcut on paper
175 x 127
P07118 (right)

EDWARD WADSWORTH 1889-1949
The Port
c1915
Woodcut print on paper
187 x 127
P07119 (right)

EDWARD WADSWORTH 1889-
1949
The Open Window
c1915
Woodcut print on paper
184 x 133
P07120 (right)

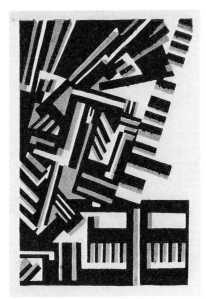

EDWARD WADSWORTH
View of a Town c1918

EDWARD WADSWORTH
The Port c1915

EDWARD WADSWORTH
The Open Window c1915

LOANS

JACOB EPSTEIN 1880-1959
'The Rock Drill' (p38)
(Reconstruction 1973-4 after loss of
original 1913-5)
Polyester resin, metal and wood
2050 x 1415 x 1415
Birmingham Museum and Art Gallery

British First World War aircraft propeller
2413 x 203 x 152
Trustees of the Imperial War Museum

German First World War aircraft propeller
2692 x 203 x 127
Trustees of the Imperial War Museum

*Four aircraft wing ribs, examples of Women's
Work in the First World War*
1714 x 102 x 13
1714 x 102 x 13
596 x 89 x 19
596 x 76 x 12
Trustees of the Imperial War Museum

*Alloy girder joint from First World War
airship*
800 x 787 x 914 at right 533 Front to
back 895
Trustees of the Imperial War Museum

*German First World War rifle-grenade
throwing rest*
742 x 444 x 1041/787
Trustees of the Imperial War Museum

*German First World War Grenatenwerfer
spigot mortar*
355 x 279 x 431
Trustees of the Imperial War Museum

*Propeller boss for First World War rotary
aircraft engine*
330 diameter x 279
Trustees of the Imperial War Museum

*First World War Period British Oliver
typewriter*
266 x 280 x 368
Trustees of the Imperial War Museum

*German First World War wall-mounted field
telephone*
349 x 203 x 177
Trustees of the Imperial War Museum

*Metal components produced by female labour
employed under the Substitution Scheme in
the First World War*
Varied dimensions
Trustees of the Imperial War Museum

ISBN 1 05437 053 7

Published by order of the Trustees for
the collection display 'Dynamism'
20 March – 29 December 1991

Prepared by Tate Gallery Liverpool,
Albert Dock, Liverpool L3 4BB
Published by Tate Gallery Publications,
Millbank, London SW1P 4RG
Edited by Penelope Curtis
Designed by Jeremy Greenwood
Printed in Great Britain by Printfine
Limited, Liverpool